Formula - one.   Sport - nil.

What a cracking year! From Damon in March, struggling to get on the grid in Melbourne to the FIA on 11 November announcing that the earth was flat, Elvis was alive and Michael Schumacher is the greatest sportsman who has ever lived. Remember it's just showbiz and in showbusiness you don't sack your star attraction!

Many thanks to the FIA for keeping the farce going and making my job so easy, and to Laurence Foster and the lads and lasses at AUTOSPORT for their many contributions. To *Cars and Car Conversions* for their continuing support – 15 years of it! *Loaded* magazine for the pics of Jo Guest and last but not least to Simon Taylor for 'coming on board' and agreeing to write the foreword knowing full well he would get hammered (see next page).

Jim Bamber
Canary Islands 1997

The Pits 5 by Jim Bamber. ISBN 0 86024 932 8. Produced by Autosport Special Projects. Published by Haymarket Specialist Publications Ltd. Repro by Primary Colours, Chiswick, London. Printed by BR Hubbard Ltd, Sheffield.

Foreword

Formula 1 is a serious business these days. Millions of pounds, hundredths of seconds, and straight faces. A sense of humour isn't a key ingredient for successful team bosses, sponsors, world champions, deal makers.

So, thank goodness for Jim Bamber. Jim has been finding F1 funny for years – and the rest of motorsport, too – both in AUTOSPORT every week, and also in some other great cartons which appear in these pages for the first time.

Quite rightly, no-one in F1 escapes. When the ITV team tried to present their Monaco GP coverage from on board the only boat in the harbour without a keel, during the roughest race-day in living memory, we weren't laughing. As is now well-known, I certainly wasn't...

With Jim's help, we can now see the funny side. In these super-professional days, he does us all a service.

The FIA and FOCA should make *The Pits 5* required reading for everyone in the sport. And they should read it themselves.

Simon Taylor
Broadcaster and Chairman of Haymarket Magazines

The new World Champion had a lot on his plate at the start of the year

Every Christmas in York Cathedral co-drivers from all over the rallying world congregate to play with their belles and to slag off their respective driving partners. At the end of '96 it was Derek Ringer's turn. Great bells Tina!

More Grist to the McRae mill!

11

'The voice of Formula One', Murray Walker, brought some welcome continuity to the 1997 ITV GP programme. Which is more than can be said for the bloody awful signature tune!

The nightmare starts here

15

I know, I know, I missed one out, but please don't ask me which one.
For anyone reading this in two years' time-McLaren hired an all girl pop group called the Spice Girls.

17

Wow! What a season! Was I right or was I right?

19

At the beginning of the year we all thought Williams would walk it

21

In 1997 Lola entered the fray but asking is one thing, getting another.
In Melbourne the cars were 11 seconds off the pace!

23

Only two races into the season reality finally caught up with Lola

There were demonstrations in Melbourne by environmentalists who showed their love
for the planet by dumping diesel oil in the park!?

27

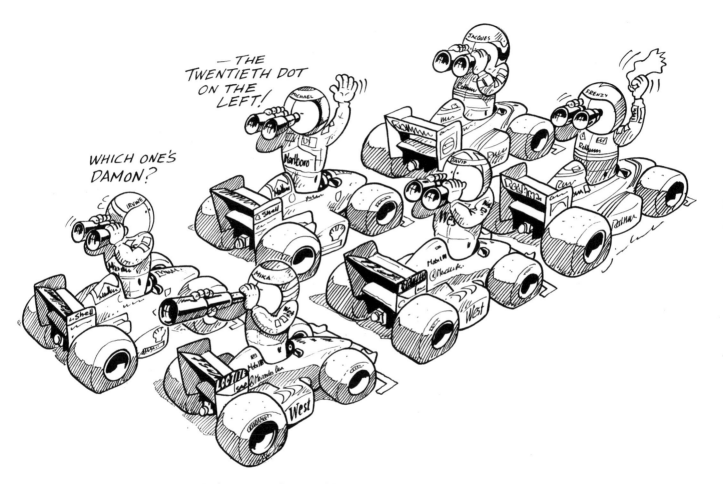

Where was the World Champion in Melbourne?

For Williams the first race of the season was a disaster...it wouldn't be the last!

In Melbourne the 'Braveheart' team had outqualified the Jordans

33

In Brazil we didn't see much in Frentzen to get excited about

With Eddie Irvine making a race of it the Argentine Grand Prix was almost
as exciting as the football that weekend....almost!

At Monaco a fantastic second place for 'Barrychello' and the Stewart team

Nearly everybody thought the Arrows open day was a great success!

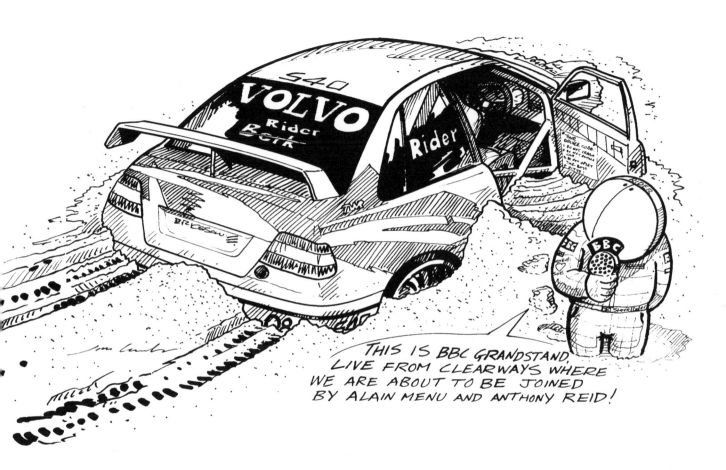

The unflappable Steve Rider trying his hand at Rallycross....in a Touring Car!

Blistering tyres were the cause of Frentzen's woes in Spain

45

No I hadn't forgotten him. Mark Blundell was driving brilliantly in America but up until Detroit he wasn't doing enough to catch my evil eye!

Alain Menu was walking away with the BTCC, the 'Boring Touring Car Championship.'

For Mark the waiting was finally over. His first CART Indycar win, great stuff.

This June, former Autosport Editor and sportscar fan Quentin Spurring and his lovely wife Jane celebrated 30 years of happy motoring

ITV's dream team Martin and 'Muddly' our dynamic duo

Amazingly the Chinese guard, top left, bears a striking resemblance to Autosport's assistant editor Henry Hope-Frost

57

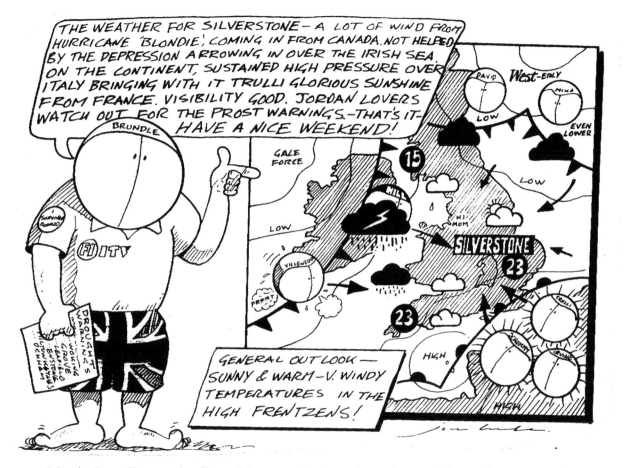

Martin Brundle was the find of the year. Informative, witty and the perfect partner for Murray. He rides a Ducati as well, what more can I say?

It's a cruel sport at times. Hakkinen wasn't the only driver denied a result at Silverstone

.....but for the struggling World Champion, sixth place and his first point
of the year was very welcome

In July I was asked by Prodrive to do a card for Colin's wedding. This one didn't make it!

In Germany we had a 100% Beefy Berger. Pole position, fastest lap, victory, the man's a star.

This is for Mark at Arrows for giving us one of 1997's magic moments....sob!

The young Lions were doing well in the BTCC or the, 'Better Try Catching Cleland' to Derek Warwick

The silly season was upon us and Damon was up for grabs.

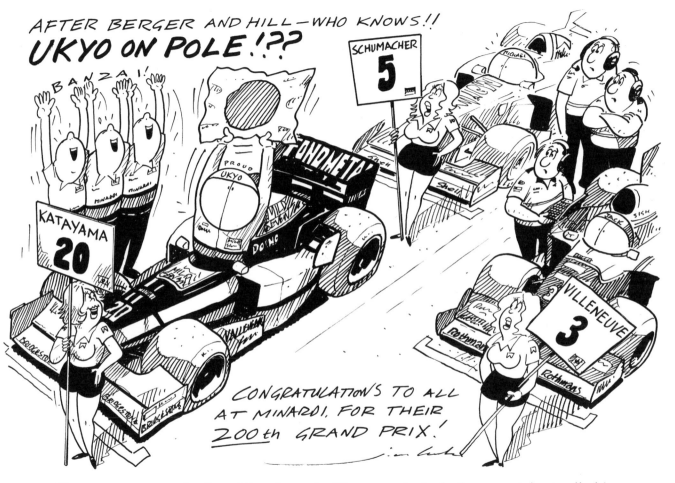

Katayama was to retire from F1 at the end of the year – he had other mountains to climb!

DAMON AT SPA — SPOILT FOR CHOICE!!

At Spa in the wet Hill finished 13th, seven places behind his team mate –
the *less* experienced Diniz.

Bizarre. Schumacher tested a Sauber during the year as a favour?
For who?

The yes yes vote in Scotland brought the haggis eaters independence, so from henceforth we can say with confidence........Partick Thistle - Free!

....and so say all of us!

The McLaren pit crew at Monza-fastest guns in the west!

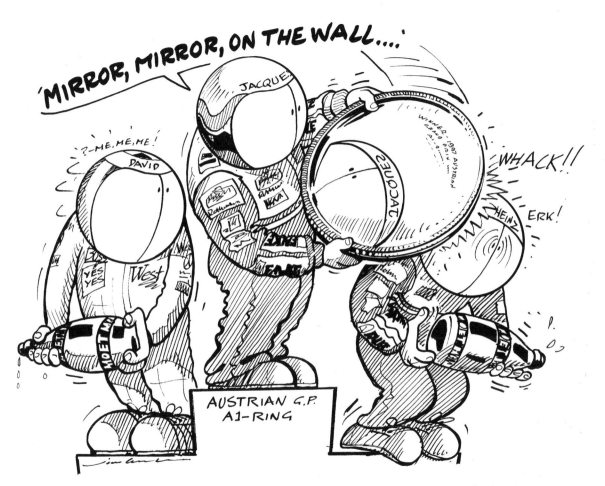

At last 'Blondie' could see his face in the World Championship mirror!

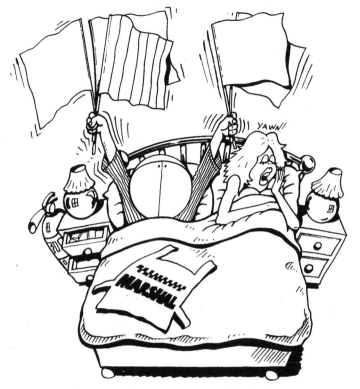

CIRCUIT MARSHALS 'ALWAYS' FLAG!

Coming soon to a t-shirt near you!

At Spa the Gulf McLaren boys enjoyed a spot of 'bonding!'

At the Nurburgring the Schumacher brothers took points off each other

93

Wilson, the legendary comic book saviour of British sport.
I never thought he existed until now

A rather one-sided tug of war

97

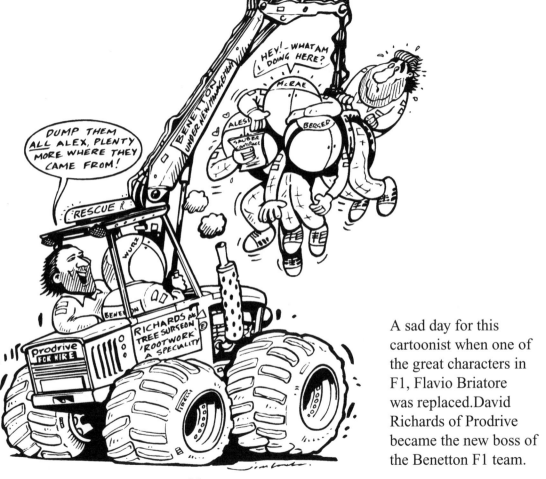

A sad day for this cartoonist when one of the great characters in F1, Flavio Briatore was replaced. David Richards of Prodrive became the new boss of the Benetton F1 team.

Fast Eddie, having to give up his first Grand Prix win to help that great sportsman......
....you know, whatsisname?

Williams had won the constructors championship while Jacques still had it all to do

England only needed a point from their match with Italy to secure a place in the 1998 World Cup Finals....

....whereas Italy **had** to win, sound familiar?

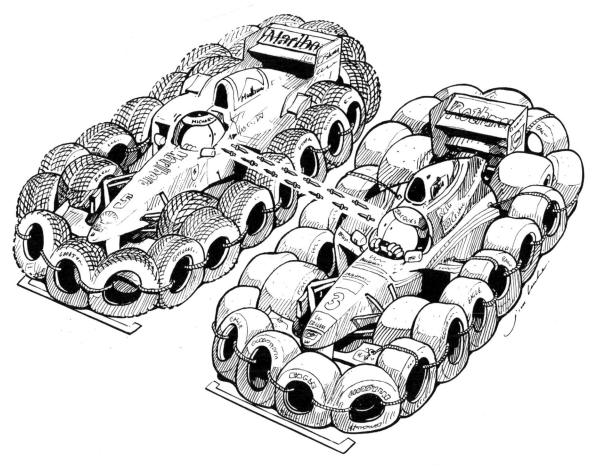

Before the final Grand Prix of the season at Jerez we all expected
a bit of argy-bargy and wow did we get it!

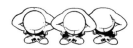

This is the moment F1 became a soap opera

FIA Stewards on their way to discuss a 'racing incident!'

Hero to zero!

Following all the talk about tobacco sponsorship the lads at
Wessex Motor Club came up with a novel idea

On their way to the Laugh-in at Colnbrook, Schumacher and Todt playing around with their tapes. Afterwards most of us were left humming 'Whiter shade of Pale!'

It was a relief to watch an event with two sportsmen worthy of the name.
The Network Q RAC Rally was upon us.

You couldn't get F1 out of the papers

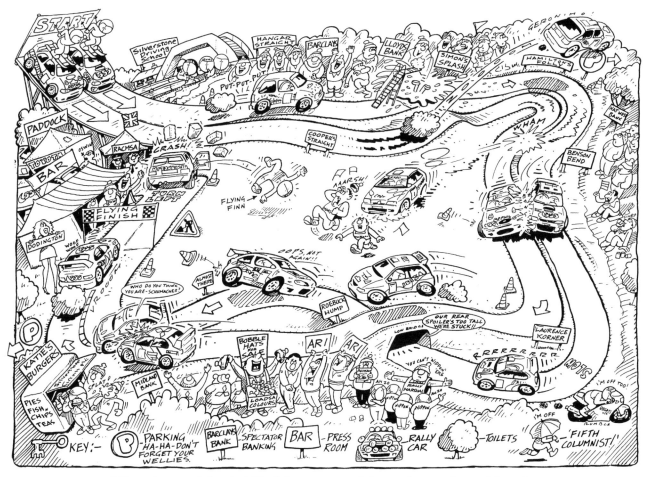

Silverstone celebrated Katie's superspecial new burger bar with style.